Congressional Research Service

Medical Marijuana: The Supremacy Clause, Federalism, and the Interplay Between State and Federal Laws

Todd Garvey
Legislative Attorney

November 9, 2012

Congressional Research Service
7-5700
www.crs.gov
R42398

CRS Report for Congress ————————————————
Prepared for Members and Committees of Congress

Summary

As part of a larger scheme to regulate drugs and other controlled substances, federal law prohibits the cultivation, distribution, and possession of marijuana. No exception is made for marijuana used in the course of a recommended medical treatment. Indeed, by categorizing marijuana as a Schedule I drug under the Controlled Substances Act (CSA), the federal government has concluded that marijuana has "no currently accepted medical use in treatment in the United States." Yet 18 states and the District of Columbia have decriminalized medical marijuana by enacting exceptions to their state drug laws that permit individuals to grow, possess, or use marijuana for medicinal purposes. In contrast to the complete federal prohibition, these 19 jurisdictions see medicinal value in marijuana and permit the drug's use under certain circumstances.

Although the U.S. Supreme Court has established Congress's constitutional authority to enact the existing federal prohibition on marijuana, principles of federalism prevent the federal government from mandating that the states actively support or participate in enforcing the federal law. While state resources may be helpful in combating the illegal use of marijuana, Congress's ability to compel the states to enact similar criminal prohibitions, to repeal medical marijuana exemptions, or to direct state police officers to enforce the federal law remains limited by the Tenth Amendment.

Even if the federal government is prohibited from mandating that the states adopt laws supportive of federal policy, the constitutional doctrine of preemption generally prevents states from enacting laws that are inconsistent with federal law. Under the Supremacy Clause, state laws that conflict with federal law are generally preempted and therefore void. Courts, however, have not viewed the relationship between state and federal marijuana laws in such a manner, nor did Congress intend that the CSA displace all state laws associated with controlled substances. Instead, the relationship between the federal ban on marijuana and state medical marijuana exemptions must be considered in the context of two distinct sovereigns, each enacting separate and independent criminal regimes with separate and independent enforcement mechanisms, in which certain conduct may be prohibited under one sovereign and not the other. Although state and federal marijuana laws may be "logically inconsistent," a decision not to criminalize—or even to expressly decriminalize—conduct for purposes of the law within one sphere does nothing to alter the legality of that same conduct in the other sphere.

This report will review the federal government's constitutional authority to enact the federal criminal prohibition on marijuana; highlight certain principles of federalism that prevent the federal government from mandating that states participate in enforcing the federal prohibition; consider unresolved questions relating to the extent to which state authorization and regulation of medical marijuana are preempted by federal law; and assess what obligations, if any, the U.S. Department of Justice (DOJ) has to investigate and prosecute violations of the federal prohibition on marijuana.

Contents

Contacts

Introduction

As part of a larger scheme to regulate drugs and other controlled substances, federal law prohibits the cultivation, distribution, and possession of marijuana.[1] No exception is made for marijuana used in the course of a recommended medical treatment. Indeed, by categorizing marijuana as a Schedule I drug under the Controlled Substances Act (CSA), the federal government has concluded that marijuana has "no currently accepted medical use in treatment in the United States."[2]

Yet 18 states and the District of Columbia have decriminalized medical marijuana by enacting exceptions to their drug laws that permit individuals to grow, possess, or use marijuana for medicinal purposes.[3] In contrast to the complete federal prohibition, these 19 jurisdictions see medicinal value in marijuana and permit the drug's use under certain circumstances. Such inconsistencies in federal and state law would generally evoke the constitutional principle of preemption—potentially resulting in a conclusion that because the states permit conduct that the federal government has expressly prohibited, such laws are void as in conflict with the "supreme law of the land."[4] This, however, has not been the case. State laws that exempt from state criminal sanctions the cultivation, distribution, or possession of marijuana for medical purposes have generally not been preempted by federal law.

This unique interplay between state and federal law has led to a seemingly incongruous situation in which both the federal criminal prohibition on marijuana and state medical marijuana exemptions coexist. Accordingly, a resident of California who uses marijuana for medical purposes in compliance with California law is nonetheless simultaneously in violation of federal law and potentially subject to prosecution by federal authorities. Such prosecutions, however, are relatively rare. The federal government has limited resources to draw upon in investigating and enforcing federal drug laws.[5] As a consequence, the Obama Administration has formally suggested that it will not prosecute individuals who use medicinal marijuana in a manner consistent with state laws.[6]

The legal anomaly that defines the use of medical marijuana in the United States raises a number of important constitutional questions—some of which have been answered by the U.S. Supreme Court, but many of which remain unresolved. This report will review the federal government's constitutional authority to enact the federal criminal prohibition on marijuana; highlight certain principles of federalism that prevent the federal government from mandating that states

---

[1] Controlled Substances Act, 21 U.S.C. §§801 et seq.

[2] 21 U.S.C. §812(b)(1).

[3] Theses states include Alaska, Arizona, California, Colorado, Connecticut, Delaware, Hawaii, Maine, Massachusetts, Michigan, Montana, Nevada, New Jersey, New Mexico, Oregon, Rhode Island, Vermont, and Washington. In addition, the state of Maryland has a medical marijuana law that permits individuals arrested for possession of one ounce of marijuana or less to raise medical use as an affirmative defense at trial. Md. Ann. Code §5-601.

[4] U.S. Const., Art. VI, cl. 2 ("The Constitution, and the Laws of the United States which shall be made in Pursuance thereof; and all Treaties made, or which shall be made, under the Authority of the United States, shall be the supreme Law of the Land.").

[5] Memorandum for selected U.S. Attorneys from David W. Ogden, Deputy Attorney General, *Investigations and Prosecutions in States Authorizing the Medical Use of Marijuana*, October 19, 2009 (hereinafter Ogden Memorandum) *available at* http://www.justice.gov/opa/documents/medical-marijuana.pdf.

[6] *Id.*

participate in enforcing the federal prohibition; consider unresolved questions relating to the extent to which state authorization and regulation of medical marijuana are preempted by federal law; and assess what obligations, if any, the U.S. Department of Justice (DOJ) has to investigate and prosecute violations of the federal prohibition on marijuana.

Legal Landscape: Federal and State Laws

Prior to considering the significant constitutional questions associated with the interplay between state and federal laws in the context of medical marijuana, the following section provides a description of the CSA and a brief discussion of common characteristics found within the wide variety of state medical marijuana laws that have been enacted across the country.

Federal Law

Enacted in 1970, the CSA establishes a statutory framework through which the federal government regulates the lawful production, possession, and distribution of controlled substances.[7] The CSA places various plants, drugs, and chemicals (such as narcotics, stimulants, depressants, hallucinogens, and anabolic steroids) into one of five schedules based on the substance's medical use, potential for abuse, and safety or dependence liability.[8] Further, the act requires persons who handle controlled substances or listed chemicals (such as drug manufacturers, wholesale distributors, doctors, hospitals, pharmacies, and scientific researchers) to register with the Drug Enforcement Administration (DEA) in DOJ, which administers and enforces the CSA.[9] Registrants must maintain detailed records of their respective controlled substance inventories, as well as establish adequate security controls to minimize theft and diversion.[10]

Marijuana is currently categorized as a Schedule I controlled substance, and is therefore subject to the most severe restrictions contained within the CSA. Schedule I drugs have "a high potential for abuse" and "no currently accepted medical use in treatment in the United States," and lack "accepted safety for use of the drug [] under medical supervisions."[11] Pursuant to the CSA, the cultivation, distribution, or possession of marijuana is a federal crime.[12] Although various factors contribute to the ultimate sentence received, the mere possession of marijuana generally constitutes a misdemeanor subject to up to one year imprisonment and a minimum fine of $1,000.[13] The cultivation or distribution of marijuana, or the possession of marijuana with the

---

[7] 21 U.S.C. §812. It should also be noted that the United States has treaty obligations to maintain effective controls over marijuana. *See, e.g.*, Single Convention on Narcotics Drugs, March 30, 1961, 18 U.S.T. 1409.

[8] 21 U.S.C. §§811-812.

[9] 21 U.S.C. §823.

[10] *See* 21 C.F.R. §1304.11(a) ("Each inventory shall contain a complete and accurate record of all controlled substances on hand ..."); *see also* 21 C.F.R. §1301.74(a) ("All applicants and registrants shall provide effective controls to guard against theft and diversion of controlled substances ...").

[11] 21 U.S.C. §812(b)(1).

[12] Very narrow exceptions to the federal prohibition do exist. For example, one may legally use marijuana if participating in an FDA approved study or participate in the Compassionate Investigational New Drug program.

[13] 21 U.S.C. §844(a).

intent to distribute, on the other hand, is subject to more severe penalties. Such conduct generally constitutes a felony subject to as much as five years imprisonment and a fine of up to $250,000.[14]

Although individuals who use medical marijuana in compliance with state law are still in violation of federal law and subject to prosecution by federal authorities at any time, the Obama Administration has announced an informal policy that suggests a federal prosecution in that situation would be unlikely. In an October 19, 2009, memorandum, Deputy Attorney General David W. Ogden provided guidance to federal prosecutors in states that have authorized the use of medical marijuana.[15] Citing a desire to make "efficient and rational use of its limited investigative and prosecutorial resources," the memorandum stated that while the "prosecution of significant traffickers of illegal drugs, including marijuana … continues to be a core priority," federal prosecutors "should not focus federal resources [] on individuals whose actions are in clear and unambiguous compliance with existing state laws providing for the medical use of marijuana."[16] The memorandum made clear, however, that "this guidance [does not] preclude investigation or prosecution, even where there is clear and unambiguous compliance with existing state law, in particular circumstances where investigation or prosecution otherwise serves important federal interests."[17]

Responding to an increase in the "commercial cultivation, sale, distribution, and use of marijuana for purported medical purposes," DOJ released a subsequent memorandum in 2011 drawing a clear distinction between the potential prosecutions of individual patients who require marijuana in the course of medical treatment and "commercial" dispensaries.[18] After noting that several jurisdictions had recently "enacted legislation to authorize multiple large-scale, privately operated industrial marijuana cultivation centers," DOJ attempted to clarify the scope of the Ogden Memorandum:

> The Ogden memorandum was never intended to shield such activities from federal enforcement action and prosecution, even where those activities purport to comply with state law. Persons who are in the business of cultivating, selling or distributing marijuana, and those who knowingly facilitate such activities, are in violation of the [CSA] regardless of state law. Consistent with resource constraints and the discretion you may exercise in your district, such persons are subject to federal enforcement action, including potential prosecution.[19]

The memorandum clearly communicated that individuals operating or "facilitating" medical marijuana dispensaries, even if operated in compliance with state law, continue to be targets for federal prosecution. As a result, the last two years have seen a reported increase in the number of federal DEA raids on dispensaries and marijuana farms and the subsequent prosecutions of those who own and operate marijuana distribution facilities.[20] Additionally, a number of states have

---

[14] 21 U.S.C. §841(b).

[15] Ogden Memorandum, *supra* note 5.

[16] *Id.* at 1-2.

[17] *Id.* at 3.

[18] Memorandum for U.S. Attorneys from James M. Cole, Deputy Attorney General, *Guidance Regarding the Ogden Memo in Jurisdictions Seeking to Authorize Marijuana for Medical Use*, October 19, 2009 (hereinafter Cole Memorandum).

[19] *Id.* at 2.

[20] William Yardley, *New Federal Crackdown Confounds States that Allow Medical Marijuana*, N.Y. Times (May 7, 2011).

abandoned legislative proposals to expand their medical marijuana programs, at least partly as a result of warnings from U.S. Attorneys that the DOJ will "vigorously" enforce the CSA against those who participate in the unlawful manufacturing or distribution of marijuana, regardless of whether such activity is licensed under state law.[21]

State Laws

Forty-eight states and the District of Columbia have criminalized the recreational use of marijuana.[22] However, beginning with California in 1996, a growing number of states have decriminalized the use of marijuana for medicinal purposes or exempted qualified users from sanctions imposed under state law. Today, 18 states and the District of Columbia have enacted provisions that, in various ways, exempt qualified individuals[23] from state criminal prosecution and various state civil penalties for marijuana-related offenses.[24] Although these laws vary widely in their approaches to medical marijuana, there are a number of common characteristics that appear to adhere to these laws. First, in order for an individual to legally use medical marijuana, the drug must have been recommended by a physician for use in treating a diagnosed medical condition.[25] All states but California require that this recommendation be in writing.[26] Most states also require potential users to register with the state.[27] Upon registration, states will often provide the user with a registration card so that the individual can be identified as a qualified user of medical marijuana.[28] Additionally, all states but California limit the quantity of marijuana that a patient may possess at any one time, and most states have laws limiting the manner and place in which a qualified individual can use the drug.[29]

Although these 19 jurisdictions have established a scheme by which qualified individuals may legally possess and use marijuana for medicinal purposes under state law, qualified users in some jurisdictions lack a legal avenue to obtain adequate quantities of the drug. Some states permit users to grow their own marijuana, while others license third-party private persons or entities to

---

[21] *See*, Chad Livengood and Doug Denison, *Medical Marijuana Law Busted*, The News Journal (Delaware), February 12, 2012; Olivia Katrandjian, *Under Federal Threat, Washington Governor Vetoes Medical Marijuana Dispensary Bill*, ABC News, April 30, 2011.

[22] On November 6, 2012, Colorado and Washington became the first states to decriminalize marijuana for recreational use. *See*, Colorado Ballot Initiative Amendment 64, *available at*: http://www.sos.state.co.us/pubs/elections/Initiatives/ titleBoard/filings/2011-2012/30Final.pdf; Washington Ballot Initiative I-502, *available at*: http://sos.wa.gov/_assets/ elections/initiatives/i502.pdf. The approved ballot initiatives legalize the possession of small amounts of marijuana and regulate and tax the drug as the state does other substances such as alcohol and tobacco. A legal analysis of these recently adopted laws is beyond the scope of this report; however, for a brief discussion of the legal issues that arise as a result of these measures, see CRS Legal Sidebar WSLG295, Can a State Really "Legalize" Marijuana, by Todd Garvey. In addition, some states and localities treat the possession of small amounts of marijuana (typically one ounce or less) as a civil, rather than criminal, offense. *See, e.g.*, Colo. Rev. Stat. §18-18-406 ("any person who possesses two ounces or less of marijuana commits a class 2 petty offense ... punished by a fine of not more than one hundred dollars.").

[23] State exemptions often apply not only to the patients, but also primary caregivers and physicians. *See, e.g.*, Nev. Rev. Stat. §453A.220.

[24] For purposes of this report, the term "state" includes the District of Columbia.

[25] *See, e.g.*, R.I. Gen Laws §21-28.6-4.

[26] California permits an "oral recommendation." Cal. Health & Safety Code §11362.5.

[27] *See, e.g.*, Wash. Rev. Code §69.51A.040.

[28] *See, e.g.*, Colo. Const. Art. XVIII §14.

[29] *See. e.g.*, Ore. Rev. Stat. §§475.316, 475.319.

---

cultivate and distribute the drug to qualified individuals through state-licensed and -regulated dispensaries.[30] California has also authorized patients and caregivers to collectively grow marijuana in "cannabis cooperatives."[31] In those states where supply is limited, however, many medical marijuana users are forced to acquire the marijuana they are permitted to possess and use through the black market.[32]

A Series of Constitutional Questions

The unique inconsistencies between federal and state approaches to medical marijuana give rise to a series of important constitutional questions. First, is it within Congress's power to prohibit the production, possession, and distribution of marijuana? Second, to what extent can the federal government direct states to adopt similar laws or enforce the federal prohibition? Third, to what extent are state attempts to authorize and regulate medical marijuana preempted by federal law? And finally, what obligation, if any, does DOJ have to enforce the federal prohibition?

Is It Within Congress's Power to Prohibit the Production, Possession, and Distribution of Marijuana?

The U.S. Supreme Court considered the reach of Congress's Commerce Clause authority and the constitutionality of the CSA in *Gonzales v. Raich*.[33] *Raich* involved a challenge to the federal marijuana prohibition brought by Angel Raich and Diane Monson after agents of the federal DEA seized and destroyed marijuana plants that Monson had been cultivating for medical purposes consistent with California law. The respondents argued that the CSA's "categorical prohibition," as applied to the "intrastate manufacture and possession of marijuana for medical purposes," exceeded Congress's authority under the Commerce Clause, and, therefore, could not serve as the basis for their prosecution.[34] The Court rejected this argument, and clearly held that the federal prohibition was within Congress's constitutional authority.

In a 6-3 decision, the Court upheld Congress's power to prohibit even the purely intrastate cultivation and possession of marijuana. Relying heavily on its 1942 decision of *Wickard v. Filburn*, the Court held that prior precedent had "firmly establish[ed] Congress'[s] power to regulate purely local activities that are part of an economic 'class of activities' that have a substantial effect on interstate commerce."[35] In enacting the CSA, Congress had sought to regulate the supply and demand of controlled substances, including marijuana. Consistent with that objective, Congress had rationally concluded that "leaving home-consumed marijuana

---

[30] *See, e.g.*, Ariz. Rev. Stat. §36-2806.02.

[31] Cal. Health & Safety Code §11362.765.

[32] *See*, Robert A. Mikos, *On the Limits of Supremacy: Medical Marijuana and the States' Overlooked Power to Legalize Federal Crime*, 62 Vand. L. Rev. 1421, 1432 (2009) ("Most states, however have simply refused or neglected to address the issue ... This means that qualified patients must often resort to the black market to obtain the marijuana they are legally entitled to possess.").

[33] 545 U.S. 1 (2005).

[34] *Id.* at 15.

[35] *Id.* at 17-18 ("The similarities between this case and *Wickard* are striking."). In Wickard v. Filburn, 317 U.S. 111 (1942), the Court held that the Agricultural Adjustment Act's federal quota system applied to bushels of wheat that were homegrown and personally consumed.

---

outside federal control" would have a "substantial effect on supply and demand in the national market" for marijuana.[36] The Court noted that even small amounts of marijuana grown at home—though intended for personal medicinal use—would likely be diverted into the national market and frustrate Congress's goal of strictly controlling overall supply.[37] Thus, in enacting the federal prohibition on marijuana production, possession, and distribution, Congress was acting "well within its authority to 'make all Laws which shall be necessary and proper' to 'regulate commerce ... among the several states.'"[38]

For purposes of this report, it is important to note that the Court's opinion in *Raich* dealt only with the question of whether the Commerce Clause permitted Congress to prohibit the wholly intrastate possession and use of marijuana. The Court did not consider the question of whether the California law, which permitted the use of marijuana for medicinal purposes, was preempted by the CSA. The Court noted only that respondents' compliance with state law in cultivating marijuana had no impact on the scope of Congress's power under the Commerce Clause, as "[i]t is beyond peradventure that federal power over commerce is 'superior to that of the States to provide for the welfare or necessities of their inhabitants,' however legitimate or dire those necessities may be."[39]

May the Federal Government Direct the States to Adopt Similar Laws or to Enforce the Federal Prohibition?

Although *Raich* established Congress's constitutional authority to enact the existing federal prohibition on marijuana, principles of federalism prevent the federal government from mandating that the states support or participate in enforcing the federal law. While state resources may be helpful in combating the illegal use of marijuana, Congress's ability to compel the states to enact similar criminal prohibitions, to repeal medical marijuana exemptions, or to direct state police officers to enforce the federal law remains limited. The Tenth Amendment likely prevents such an intrusion into state sovereignty.

The Tenth Amendment provides that the "powers not delegated to the United States by the Constitution, nor prohibited by it to the States, are reserved to the States respectively, or to the people."[40] Initially, the Supreme Court interpreted the Tenth Amendment as establishing that certain "core" state functions would be beyond the authority of the federal government to regulate.[41] The Court's interpretation of the Tenth Amendment soon shifted, however, from protecting "core" state functions to preventing the federal government from "commandeering" state government.[42] In *New York v. United States*, the Court struck down a federal statute that had mandated that states either develop legislation on how to dispose of all low-level radioactive waste generated within their borders, or be forced to take title to such waste and become

---

[36] *Raich*, 545 U.S. at 19.

[37] *Id.* ("[T]he diversion of homegrown marijuana tends to frustrate the federal interest in eliminating commercial transactions in the interstate market in their entirety.").

[38] *Id.* at 22.

[39] *Id.* at 29.

[40] U.S. Const. amend. X ("The powers not delegated to the United States by the Constitution, nor prohibited by it to the States, are reserved to the States respectively, or to the people.").

[41] National League of Cities v. Usery, 426 U.S. 833 (1976).

[42] New York v. United States, 505 U.S. 144 (1992).

responsible for any financial consequences.[43] The Court found that although Congress had the authority under the Commerce Clause to regulate low-level radioactive waste, it had only the power to regulate the waste directly—Congress could not require that the states perform the regulation rather than regulate the waste directly itself. In effect, Congress could not "commandeer" the legislative process of the states.[44]

Nor may Congress "commandeer" state executive branch officers for purposes of carrying out or enforcing federal law. In *Printz v. United States*, the Supreme Court invalidated a provision of the Brady Handgun Violence Prevention Act that had required that state police officers conduct background checks on prospective handgun purchasers within five days of an attempted purchase.[45] The Court held that the provision constituted an unconstitutional "commandeering" of state officers and, like a commandeering of the legislature, was outside of Congress's power and a violation of the Tenth Amendment.[46]

Consistent with *New York v. United States* and *Printz*, the federal government is prohibited from commandeering state legislatures or state executive officials by mandating that states enact certain legislation or implement or enforce a federal law.[47] Given these restrictions, Congress may not statutorily direct that states enact complete prohibitions on marijuana or repeal existing exemptions for medical marijuana. Nor may Congress direct that state police officers enforce the marijuana provisions of the CSA. Congress may, however, be able to persuade states to support the federal policy by conditioning the receipt of federal funds upon the state enacting legislation consistent with the CSA.[48] In addition, states may voluntarily alter their own laws or enforce federal laws, but they cannot be made to do so by the federal government.[49]

To What Extent Are State Medical Marijuana Laws Preempted by Federal Law?

Even if the federal government is prohibited from mandating that the states adopt laws supportive of federal policy, the constitutional doctrine of preemption generally prevents states from enacting laws that are inconsistent with federal law. Thus, the federal government typically stands on much stronger constitutional footing when it attempts to stop a state action than when it attempts to force a state to act.

At first glance, it would appear that a state law that permits an activity expressly prohibited by federal law would necessarily create a legal "conflict" between state and federal law. Under the Supremacy Clause, state laws that conflict with federal law are generally preempted and therefore

---

[43] *Id.*

[44] *Id.* at 175.

[45] 521 U.S. 898 (1997).

[46] *Id.* at 904-918.

[47] In *Reno v. Condon*, the Supreme Court held that a federal law does not "commandeer" state resources so long as it "does not require the States in their sovereign capacities to regulate their own citizens," but rather regulates state activities directly. 528 U.S. 141, 151 (2000).

[48] *See*, South Dakota v. Dole, 483 U.S. 203 (1987); *New York*, 505 U.S. at 188 (pointing out that the Spending Clause provides an alternative to the congressional "commandeering" of state officials that violated the Tenth Amendment).

[49] See, Printz v. United States, 521 U.S. 898, 933, 138 L. Ed. 2d 914, 117 S. Ct. 2365 (1997) (O'Connor, J., concurring) (discussing ability of state officials to voluntarily continue to participate in a federal program).

---

void.[50] Courts, however, have not viewed the relationship between state and federal marijuana laws in such a manner, nor did Congress intend that the CSA displace all state laws associated with controlled substances.[51] Instead, the relationship between the federal ban on marijuana and state medical marijuana exemptions must be considered in the context of two distinct sovereigns, each enacting separate and independent criminal regimes with separate and independent enforcement mechanisms, in which certain conduct may be prohibited under one sovereign and not the other. Although state and federal marijuana laws may be "logically inconsistent," a decision not to criminalize—or even to expressly decriminalize—conduct for purposes of the law within one sphere does nothing to alter the legality of that same conduct in the other sphere.

Preemption is grounded in the Supremacy Clause of Article VI, cl. 2, which states that "[t]he Constitution, and the Laws of the United States which shall be made in Pursuance thereof; and all Treaties made, or which shall be made, under the Authority of the United States, shall be the supreme Law of the Land."[52] The Supremacy Clause, therefore, "elevates" the U.S. Constitution, federal statutes, federal regulations, and ratified treaties above the laws of the states.[53] As a result, where a state law is in conflict with a federal law, the federal law must prevail. There is, however, a presumption against federal preemption when it comes to the exercise of "historic police powers of the States."[54] State medical marijuana laws have generally been accorded this presumption, as they are enacted pursuant to traditional state police powers in defining criminal conduct and regulating drugs and medical practices.

Although there is "no one crystal clear distinctly marked formula" for determining whether a state law is preempted by federal law, the Supreme Court has established three general classes of preemption: express preemption, conflict preemption, and field preemption.[55] In each instance, however, "the question of preemption is one of determining congressional intent."[56] Express preemption exists where the language of a federal statute explicitly states the degree to which related state laws are superseded by the federal statute.[57] Where, in contrast, Congress does not articulate its view as to a statute's intended impact on state laws, a court may *imply* preemption if there is evidence that Congress intended to supplant state authority.[58] Preemption is generally implied in two situations. First, under conflict preemption, a state law is preempted "where compliance with both federal law and state regulations is a physical impossibility ... or where state law stands as an obstacle to the accomplishment and execution of the full purposes and objectives of Congress."[59] Thus, where one cannot simultaneously comply with both state and

---

[50] *See, e.g.*, Wickard v. Filburn, 317 U.S. 111, 124 (1942)("[N]o form of state activity can constitutionally thwart the regulatory power granted by the commerce clause to Congress").

[51] 21 U.S.C. §903 (limiting the preemptive scope of the CSA to only those state laws that create a "positive conflict" with federal law).

[52] U.S. Const., Art. VI, cl. 2.

[53] Northern States Power Co. v. Minnesota, 447 F.2d 1143, 1145 (8th Cir. 1971).

[54] Rice v. Santa Fe Elevator Corp., 331 U.S. 218, 230 (1947).

[55] Hines v. Davidowitz, 312 U.S. 52, 67 (1941); *See also*, English v. General Elec. Co., 496 U.S. 72, 79 (1990) ("By referring to these three categories, we should not be taken to mean that they are rigidly distinct.").

[56] Skull Valley Band of Goshute Indians v. Nielson, 376 F.3d 1223, 1240 (10th Cir. 2004) (citing Wardair Canada, Inc. v. Florida Dep't of Revenue 477 U.S. 1 (1986)).

[57] *See, e.g.*, Norfolk & Western Ry. v. American Train Dispatchers' Ass'n, 499 U.S. 117 (1991).

[58] However, where Congress legislates in an area displacing "the historic police powers of the States," courts should imply preemption only where it is the "clear and manifest purpose of Congress." Rice v. Santa Fe Elevator Corp., 331 U.S. 218, 230 (1947).

[59] *See*, Gade v. National Solid Waste Management Assn., 505 U.S. 88, 98 (1992).

---

federal law, or where the state law directly frustrates the purpose of a federal law, the state law is preempted. Second, under field preemption, a state law is preempted where a "scheme of federal regulation is so pervasive as to make reasonable the inference that Congress left no room for the States to supplement it...."[60]

The CSA contains a statutory preemption provision that expressly articulates Congress's intent as to the relationship between state and federal law and the extent to which the latter displaces the former. Section 903 states:

> No provision of this subchapter shall be construed as indicating an intent on the part of the Congress to occupy the field in which that provision operates, including criminal penalties, to the exclusion of any State law on the same subject matter which would otherwise be within the authority of the State, *unless there is a positive conflict between that provision of this subchapter and that State law so that the two cannot consistently stand together.*[61]

The CSA's preemptive effect is therefore limited to only those state laws that are in "positive conflict" with the CSA such that the two "cannot consistently stand together."[62] Notably, the provision clarifies that Congress did not intend to entirely occupy the regulatory field concerning controlled substances or wholly supplant traditional state authority in the area. Indeed, Congress expressly declined to assert field preemption as grounds for preempting state law under the CSA. Arguably, then, the preemptive effect of the CSA is not as broad as congressional authority could have allowed. States remain free to pass laws relating to marijuana, or other controlled substances, so long as they do not create a "positive conflict" with federal law. In interpreting this provision, courts have generally established that a state medical marijuana law is in "positive conflict" with the CSA if it is "physically impossible" to comply with both the state and federal law, or where the state law "stands as an obstacle to the accomplishment and execution of the full purposes and objectives of Congress."[63]

CSA Preemption as Applied to State Medical Marijuana Exemptions

Both federal and state courts have consistently held that a state's decision to exempt certain classes of individuals from the state prohibition on marijuana by permitting the drug's use for medicinal purposes does not create a "positive conflict" with federal law. A mere exemption from state prosecution neither (1) makes it "impossible to comply" with both state and federal law nor (2) "stands as an obstacle" to the execution of Congress's objectives.

The "impossibility" prong of conflict preemption has traditionally been viewed very narrowly. The Supreme Court has consistently held that there is no basis to imply impossibility preemption where a state simply *permits* what the federal government *prohibits*.[64] So long as an individual is not compelled to engage in conduct prohibited by federal law, then simultaneous compliance with

---

[60] *Santa Fe Elevator Corp.*, 331 U.S. at 230 (1947).

[61] 21 U.S.C. §903 (emphasis added).

[62] *Id.*

[63] *See, e.g.*, Emerald Steel Fabricators, Inc., v. Bureau of Labor and Industries, 348 Ore. 159 (2010); *But see*, County of San Diego v. San Diego Norml, 165 Cal. App. 4th 798 (2008)(holding that a state law conflicts with the CSA only where it is impossible to comply with both the state and federal law.).

[64] *See*, Wyeth v. Levine, 555 U.S. 555 (2009); Barnett Bank v. Nelson, 517 U.S. 25 (1996).

both laws is not impossible.[65] In the medical marijuana context, an individual can comply with the CSA and a state medical marijuana exemption by refraining from the use of marijuana altogether. Under established precedent, it would appear that the federal prohibition on marijuana would only preempt a state medical marijuana law under the impossibility prong of conflict preemption if the state law *required* individuals to use medical marijuana. State laws, of course, contain no such mandate.

The second prong of the conflict preemption analysis is broader in scope. State laws may be deemed to be in conflict with federal law if the state law "stands as an obstacle to the accomplishment and execution of the full purposes and objectives of Congress."[66] In applying this test, the Supreme Court has stated that a reviewing court must consider congressional intent and the "purposes and objectives" of the federal statute as a whole.[67] "If the purpose of the act cannot otherwise be accomplished," the Court has held, then "the state law must yield to the regulation of Congress ..."[68] Additionally, the Court has established that in areas of traditional state concern—an area within which medical marijuana laws likely fall—there exists a presumption against preemption.[69] In these areas, a more "significant" conflict may be required before a state law constitutes an obstacle to the achievement of the federal goal.[70]

Courts have generally viewed state medical marijuana exemptions as having only a limited impact on the federal government's ability to achieve its purpose of combating the use of marijuana pursuant to the CSA. An exemption from prosecution under state law does not obstruct the federal government's ability to investigate and prosecute an individual for a violation of federal law.[71] Federal courts have consistently held that compliance with state medical marijuana laws is no defense, and provides no immunity to a federal criminal prosecution under the CSA.[72] Indeed, in hearing a prosecution under federal law, at least one federal court has gone so far as to exclude the introduction of any evidence relating to the defendant's compliance with state medical marijuana provisions.[73]

While an argument can be made that the decriminalization of medical marijuana under state law represents an "obstacle to the accomplishment ... of the full purposes and objectives of Congress" by creating confusion as to the permissible uses of marijuana, it is not the case that the federal objectives "cannot otherwise be accomplished" in the face of state medical marijuana

---

[65] *Barnett Bank*, 517 U.S. at 31. (holding that a federal statute that permitted national banks to sell insurance and a state statute that prohibited banks from selling insurance did not "impose directly conflicting duties").

[66] Freightliner Corp. v. Myrick, 514 U.S. 280, 287 (1947).

[67] Crosby v. National Foreign Trade Council, 530 U.S. 363, 373 (2000)(In considering obstacle preemption, a court's judgment is to be informed by "examining the federal statute as a whole and identifying its purpose and intended effects.").

[68] *Id.*

[69] Rice v. Santa Fe Elevator Corp., 331 U.S. 218 (1947).

[70] County of San Diego v. San Diego Norml, 165 Cal. App. 4th 798 (2008) (citing Boyle v. United Technologies Corp., 487 U.S. 500, 507 (1988)).

[71] *See, e.g.*, United States v. Oakland Cannabis Buyers' Cooperative, 532 U.S. 483 (2001)(holding that there is no medical necessity defense under the CSA, even where state law recognizes such a defense.) United States v. Stacy, 734 F. Supp. 2d 1074 (S.D. Cal. 2010); United States v. Lynch, 2010 U.S. Dist. LEXIS 53011(C.D. Cal. 2010).

[72] *Stacy*, 734 F. Supp. at 1079 ("[T[he fact that an individual may not be prosecuted under [state] law does not provide him or her with immunity under federal law."); United states v. Rosenthal, 454 F.3d 943 (9th Cir. 2006) (holding that state medical marijuana law could not act as a shield to federal prosecution.)

[73] *Stacy*, 734 F. Supp. at 1084.

exemptions.[74] The federal government is still free to expend its own resources to implement and enforce its own law. Moreover, if a state decision to not criminalize conduct otherwise prohibited by federal law qualified as an obstacle to the accomplishment of federal objectives, then obstacle preemption would effectively amount to an impermissible "license to commandeer state or local resources" by denying states the ability to treat certain conduct differently than the federal government.[75]

CSA Preemption as Applied to State Authorizations of Medical Marijuana

With most state medical marijuana exemptions surviving preemption challenges, various states have utilized the resulting momentum to attempt to exert increased state control over the use of medical marijuana within their borders. As a result, some state laws have evolved from merely exempting qualified individuals from prosecution under state drug laws, to affirmatively authorizing and regulating the use of medical marijuana. For example, whereas California's initial medical marijuana law only decriminalized the use of marijuana for medicinal purposes, the state expanded its law in 2003 under the Medical Marijuana Program Act.[76] The law required that the California Department of Public Health establish a voluntary registration and identification system, under which all California counties were required to issue state identification cards to qualified applicants.[77] The law also authorized qualified individuals and primary caregivers to possess up to 8 ounces of marijuana and 6 mature marijuana plants—a provision that was later struck down by the California Supreme Court.[78] Moreover, California now permits the formation of cooperatives through which qualified individuals can cultivate and distribute marijuana.[79]

Although it is difficult to determine the extent to which states can legalize and regulate medical marijuana, laws that exceed a decision not to criminalize specific conduct, and instead actively authorize the use of marijuana in contravention of the CSA, would appear to raise more stark preemption concerns. For example, a state law that attempted to immunize its citizens from federal prosecution would be preempted as a direct obstacle to the accomplishment of federal objectives. So, too, would a state law that sought to protect its citizens from the consequences of marijuana use, such as potential disqualification from public housing, under other federal statutes.[80] Additionally, a strong argument can probably be made that if a state were to enact a law through which the state itself cultivated and distributed marijuana to qualified individuals, such a law would also be preempted.[81] Whether other, less intrusive, state laws may also be preempted remains uncertain.

---

[74] *See, Crosby*, 530 U.S. at 373.

[75] Qualified Patients Assoc. v. City of Anaheim, 187 Cal. App. 4th 734 (2010) (citing Conant v. Walters, 309 F.3d 629, 646 (9th Cir. 2002) (Kozinski, J. concurring) ("That patients may be more likely to violate federal law if the additional deterrent of state liability is removed may worry the federal government, but the proper response—according to *New York* and *Printz*—is to ratchet up the federal regulatory regime, *not* to commandeer that of the state.").

[76] Cal. Health & Safety Code §11362.5.

[77] *Id.*

[78] People v. Kelly, 222 P.3d 186 (Cal. 2010).

[79] Cal. Health & Safety Code §11362.765.

[80] *See,* Assenberg, et al. v. Anacortes Housing Authority, 2006 U.S. Dist. LEXIS 34002 (W.D. Wash. 2006)("[T]o the extent that the state law legalizes marijuana use and prohibits the forfeiture of public housing, it conflicts with the CSA and the federal statutes and regulations that criminalize marijuana use and prohibit illegal drug use in public housing.").

[81] *Mikos, supra* note 32 at 1457-59 ("A handful of states have proposed supplying marijuana directly to qualified patients via state-operated farms and distribution centers ... The CSA, however, clearly preempts any such state (continued...)

It does not appear that any federal court has engaged in a substantial discussion of the preemption issues associated with these increasingly expansive state laws.[82] However, in order to highlight the difficulty in delineating the preemptive scope of the CSA, it may be helpful to consider two state cases reviewing the California and Oregon state registration and identification card programs. These laws permit a qualified individual to register with the state and receive an identification card that is used to identify the individual as one who is permitted to cultivate or possess marijuana.[83] In analyzing whether this type of law is preempted by the CSA, the California and Oregon courts have reached very different results.

State-Issued Identification Card Program Not Preempted

In *County of San Diego v. San Diego Norml*, a California appellate court upheld the registration and identification card provisions of the California Medical Marijuana Program Act (MMPA).[84] Challenging the law, San Diego County argued that the provisions of the MMPA which required the county to issue identification cards to qualified patients and primary caregivers were preempted by the CSA and therefore without effect.[85]

In considering the preemption issue, the California court first attempted to define the preemptive scope of the CSA. Interpreting Section 903 of the CSA, the court concluded that Congress had demonstrated its intent to reject both express and field preemption—leaving only conflict preemption as sufficient to preempt a state marijuana law.[86] Notably, after considering the previously discussed "impossibility" and "obstacle" prongs of conflict preemption, the court concluded that the language of the CSA suggested that Congress "did not intend to supplant all laws posing some conceivable obstacle to the purposes of the CSA."[87] Thus, the court rejected the application of "obstacle" preemption under the CSA and held that a state law should only be preempted if it were impossible to simultaneously comply with both state and federal law.

Although determining that obstacle preemption was not applicable under the CSA, the court went on to hold that even if Congress had intended to preempt state laws that made compliance with federal law impossible or that represented an obstacle to the achievement of federal objectives, the California identification laws would still not be preempted under either standard.[88] In reaching this conclusion, the court noted that the identification cards did not "insulate the bearer from federal laws," nor did the card "imply the holder is immune from prosecution for federal

---

(...continued)

program.). Professor Mikos notes that both Maine and New Mexico have "seriously considered supplying marijuana directly to qualified patients through state-run distribution centers." *Id.* at 1432.

[82] State courts in states with medical marijuana laws have been at the forefront of marijuana preemption litigation. Some of these cases arise as a result of localities challenging state medical marijuana laws—and the obligations those laws place on the localities—as preempted under the CSA. *See, e.g.*, City of Riverside v. Inland Empire Patient's Health and Wellness Center, Inc., 200 Cal. App. 4th 885 (2011), review granted, 2012 Cal. LEXIS 1028 (Cal. January 18, 2012).

[83] Cal. Health & Safety Code §11362.71; Ore. Rev. Stat. §475.306.

[84] 165 Cal. App. 4th 798 (2008), review denied 2008 Cal. LEXIS 12220 (Cal. 2008).

[85] *Id.* at 808-809.

[86] *Id.* at 819 ("Congress intended to reject express and field preemption of state laws concerning controlled substances.").

[87] *Id.* at 823.

[88] *Id.* at 826-28.

---

offenses."[89] The identification cards, the court reasoned, instead represented a "mechanism" by which California law enforcement officers could efficiently identify those individuals who are exempted from prosecution under California law for their use of marijuana.[90]

State-Issued Identification Card Program Preempted

Contrary to the California holding, in *Emerald Steel Fabricators v. Bureau of Labor and Industries*, the Oregon Supreme Court concluded that similar identification card provisions in the Oregon Medical Marijuana Act were in "positive conflict" with the CSA and therefore preempted.[91] Under Oregon law, the state issues qualified individuals identification cards that authorize the individual to "engage in the medical use ... of marijuana" without the threat of state prosecution.[92] The challenge to the law arose in the context of an employment discrimination claim in which an employee, who had obtained an identification card due to a medical condition, was allegedly discharged for admitting that he used marijuana.[93] Oregon law requires that employers "make reasonable accommodations" for an employee's disability as long as such an accommodation does not impose an undue hardship upon the employer.[94] However, the law is to be interpreted consistently with the federal Americans with Disabilities Act, which does not afford protections for employees "currently engaged in the illegal use of drugs."[95] Although the employee's use of marijuana was legal under state law, the employer argued that the medicinal use of marijuana remains illegal under federal law and that "to the extent that [Oregon law] affirmatively authorizes the use of medical marijuana, federal law preempts that subsection ..."[96]

Unlike the California court, the Oregon Supreme Court concluded that if a state law fell within either the "impossibility" prong or the "obstacle" prong of the conflict preemption analysis, then the state law would be preempted by the CSA.[97] Noting that the Supreme Court has applied the impossibility prong of the analysis "narrowly," the court first determined that an individual could simultaneously comply with both the state and federal law by refraining from the use of marijuana.[98] However, in turning to the obstacle prong, the court held that because the Oregon law "affirmatively authorized the use of medical marijuana," it was preempted by the CSA. The court reasoned that while the law did not prevent the federal government from enforcing its own laws against Oregon users, by "affirmatively authorizing a use that federal law prohibits," the Oregon law "stands as an obstacle to the implementation and execution of the full purposes and

---

[89] *Id.* at 825.

[90] *Id.* at 827. In what may be interpreted as a limiting paragraph, the court also noted that "[a]lthough California's decision to enact statutory exemptions from state criminal prosecution for such persons arguably undermines the goals or is inconsistent with the CSA—a question we do not decide here—any alleged 'obstacle' to the federal goals is presented by those California statutes that create the exemptions, not by the statutes providing a system for rapidly identifying exempt individuals.").

[91] 348 Ore. 159 (2010).

[92] *Id.* at 525.

[93] *Id.* at 520-22.

[94] O.R.S. §659A.112.

[95] *Emerald Steel*, 348 Ore. at 521.

[96] *Id.* at 526.

[97] *Id.* at 527-28.

[98] *Id.* at 528 ("To be sure, the two laws are logically inconsistent; state law authorizes what federal law prohibits. However, a person can comply with both laws by refraining from any use of marijuana ...").

---

objectives of the Controlled Substances Act."[99] Although the court concluded that the state provisions that exempted medical marijuana users from criminal liability were within the states' authority and beyond the reach of Congress under the Tenth Amendment, the licensing provision—which authorizes an individual with an identification card to engage in the use of marijuana—was distinguishable.[100] "There is no dispute," held the court, "that Congress has the authority under the Supremacy Clause to preempt state laws that affirmatively authorize the use of medical marijuana."[101]

County of San Diego and *Emerald Steel* display the apparent ambiguities associated with delineating the degree to which states can address medical marijuana within their borders. These cases highlight a number of important questions that may play a significant role in how other courts approach these preemption questions. First, will other courts adopt the Oregon Supreme Court's distinction between a permissible "exemption" and an impermissible "authorization"?[102] If so, the consequences of such an approach could be significant. Second, should state licensing laws be characterized as an affirmative state authorization to use marijuana, or merely a mechanism by which state law enforcement officers can identify a specific class of individuals who qualify for the state medical marijuana exemption? These questions, and others, remain unresolved. However, even if state laws were not preempted, the growth of state medical marijuana laws will likely still be limited by the degree to which the federal government is willing to prosecute violations of the CSA.

Liability for State Officials?

It should be noted that state laws that provide a mechanism by which state officials who participate in helping qualified individuals gain access to marijuana may theoretically expose those state officials to federal criminal liability. It is not only individuals who possess, produce, or distribute marijuana who are subject to federal sanctions, but also those who conspire, aid and abet, or assist in that proscribed conduct.[103] Take for example, state laws that require state officials to return marijuana improperly seized from a qualified individual.[104] Theoretically, the action of returning that marijuana would qualify as a felony distribution of marijuana under the CSA. Although the CSA contains language that may act to protect state officials, the precise impact of the provision remains unclear. Section 885 provides that "no civil or criminal liability shall be imposed ... upon any duly authorized officer of any state ... who shall be lawfully engaged in the enforcement of any law ... relating to controlled substances."[105] This provision may provide protections for state officials carrying out state-directed actions that are in contravention of the CSA.[106]

---

[99] *Id.* at 529.

[100] *Id.* at 530 ("[T]he validity of the exemptions and the validity of the authorization turn on different constitutional principles.").

[101] *Id.*

[102] Additionally, how important is the fact that *Emerald Steel* arose in an employment discrimination dispute? Would the Court have reached the same conclusion if the case arose in a different context?

[103] *See, e.g.*, 21 U.S.C. §846 (making it illegal to conspire to violate the CSA); 18 U.S.C. §§2-4, 371.

[104] *See, e.g.*, Ore. Rev. Stat. §475.323.

[105] 21 U.S.C. §885(d).

[106] *See*, State v. Karma, 39 P.3d 866 (Or. App. 2002)(finding immunity for city police). If a state officer is acting pursuant to a preempted state medical marijuana provision, it is an open question as to whether he be "lawfully engaged in the enforcement of any law ..."

In contrast, however, the U.S. Attorneys for the Eastern and Western Districts of Washington State have expressly noted that state officials could be subject to prosecution under federal law for carrying out aspects of a state medical marijuana program that violates the CSA.[107] In response to a request for DOJ's position on a proposed expansion to the medical marijuana laws of Washington State, these U.S. Attorneys suggested that "state employees who conducted activities mandated by the Washington legislative proposals would not be immune from liability under the CSA."[108] The letter reportedly played a role in the governor's decision to veto the proposal.

The state of Arizona recently asked a federal district court to resolve the state officer immunity question. Partially out of concern for the potential criminal liability of state employees who implement state law, the governor of Arizona sought guidance from the Arizona United States Attorney's Office on whether the Arizona Medical Marijuana Act created a "safe harbor" from federal prosecution under the CSA. Although not referencing state employees specifically, the U.S. Attorney for the District of Arizona responded with a letter informing the governor that "growing, distributing, and possessing marijuana violates federal law no matter what state law permits," and that "compliance with state law does not create a 'safe harbor.'"[109]

The state filed suit in the U.S. District Court for the District of Arizona, asking the court for a declaratory judgment as to whether the state law created a safe harbor for state officials under the CSA. Without reaching the merits, the court dismissed the claim as unripe, holding that the state could not show that officials were "subject to a genuine threat of imminent prosecution."[110] In reaching this holding, the court specifically noted that plaintiffs had failed to "detail any history of prosecution of state employees for participation in state medical marijuana licensing schemes."[111]

What Obligation, If Any, Does the U.S. Department of Justice Have to Enforce the Federal Prohibition on Marijuana?

Although the production, possession, or distribution of marijuana is a crime under federal law, DOJ has broad discretion in deciding whether to prosecute specific violations of the law. As previously discussed, DOJ has announced a policy that federal prosecutors "should not focus federal resources [] on individuals whose actions are in clear and unambiguous compliance with existing state laws providing for the medical use of marijuana."[112] Although recognizing that the conduct remains a violation of federal law, DOJ appears to have made a decision that prosecuting individual patients who are using marijuana for medicinal purposes is not an agency priority.

---

[107] Letter from Jenny A. Durkan, U.S. Attorney for the Western District of Washington and Michael C. Ormsby, U.S. Attorney for the Eastern District of Washington, to the Honorable Christine Gregoire, Washington State Governor, April 14, 2011.

[108] *Id.*

[109] Arizona v. United States, Case No. CV 11-1072-PHX-SRB (D.C. Ariz. January 4, 2012) at 3. Governors of five other states have reportedly received similar letters. William Yardley, *New Federal Crackdown Confounds States that Allow Medical Marijuana*, N.Y. Times (May 7, 2011).

[110] Arizona v. United States, Case No. CV 11-1072-PHX-SRB (D.C. Ariz. January 4, 2012) at 7.

[111] *Id.* at 8.

[112] Ogden Memorandum, *supra* note 5 at 1-2.

The established doctrine of "prosecutorial discretion" provides the federal government with "broad discretion" as to when, whom, and whether to prosecute for violations of federal law.[113] In granting this discretion, the courts have recognized that the "decision to prosecute is particularly ill-suited to judicial review," as it involves the consideration of factors—such as the strength of evidence, deterrence value, and existing enforcement priorities—"not readily susceptible to the kind of analysis the courts are competent to undertake."[114] Although prosecutorial discretion is subject to very few limitations, it is not "unfettered." For example, the selection of whom to prosecute is subject to the non-discrimination restrictions of the Equal Protection Clause.[115] Accordingly, prosecutors cannot base a decision to prosecute on "an unjustifiable standard such as race, religion, or other arbitrary classification."[116]

A decision by an individual prosecutor not to bring charges against an individual for violating the CSA's prohibition on the production, possession, or distribution of marijuana—assuming that decision is not grounded in a discriminatory purpose—would clearly fall within the umbrella of "prosecutorial discretion." Thus, there would appear to be no constitutional defect in a prosecutor's decision not to investigate or prosecute individuals who use marijuana for medicinal purposes in compliance with state law. DOJ has no obligation to prosecute all violations of federal law.[117]

Given DOJ's position, questions may be raised as to the extent to which DOJ may decline to enforce a duly enacted federal statute. For example, a formal decision to never prosecute specific conduct that Congress has expressly disallowed may raise constitutional concerns under the separation of powers.[118] However, DOJ's position, as established in the Ogden Memorandum, does not appear to rise to such a repudiation of existing laws—either in its form or its scope. Rather, the decision to limit prosecutions appears to be based on enforcement priorities and the allocation of resources. Indeed, the Ogden Memorandum, in conjunction with the later Cole Memorandum, specifically states that the DOJ will continue to prosecute certain violations and, in fact, has done so.

Conclusion

The legal status of state laws respecting the use of medical marijuana remains ambiguous. Although state laws that merely exempt qualified users of medical marijuana from state prosecution have consistently survived preemption challenges, state laws that affirmatively authorize and regulate medical marijuana may pose a more serious "obstacle" to the accomplishment of federal objectives. Notwithstanding the many unresolved questions of preemption, this interplay between state and federal law has prompted a unique legal result. While an individual may be able to possess, distribute, or cultivate marijuana for limited purposes

---

[113] United States v. Goodwin, 457 U.S. 368, 380 (1982).

[114] Wayte v. United States, 470 U.S. 598, 607 (1985).

[115] United States v. Batchelder, 442 U.S. 114, 125 (1979).

[116] Oyler v. Boles, 368 U.S. 448, 456 (1962).

[117] *Batchelder*, 442 U.S. at 124 ("Whether to prosecute ... [is a] decision[] that generally rest[s] in the prosecutor's discretion.").

[118] The President has the constitutional obligation to "take care that the laws be faithfully executed." U.S. Const. Art II, §3. Moreover, although the effect of the provision is debated, 28 U.S.C. §547 directs that "except as otherwise provided by law, each United States attorney, within his district, shall—prosecute for all offenses against the United States ..."

under state law, that same conduct remains a criminal offense under federal law. For example, operators of licensed marijuana dispensaries—which may represent legitimate licensed business ventures under state law—are subject to felony prosecutions under federal law at any time. Thus, it appears that it is generally the discretionary restraint of the federal government, in addition to the necessity to prioritize limited resources, that brings some modicum of stability to the interplay between state medical marijuana laws and the federal prohibition on the production, possession, and distribution of marijuana.

Author Contact Information

Todd Garvey
Legislative Attorney
tgarvey@crs.loc.gov, 7-0174